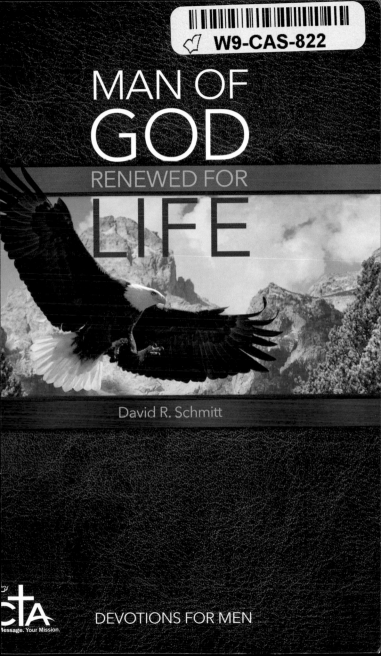

MAN OF
GOD
RENEWED FOR
LIFE

David R. Schmitt

DEVOTIONS FOR MEN

The mission of CTA is
to glorify God by providing purposeful products
that lift up and encourage the body of Christ—
because we love him.

MAN OF
GOD
RENEWED FOR
LIFE

David R. Schmitt

Copyright © 2017 CTA, Inc.
1625 Larkin Williams Rd.
Fenton, MO 63026

www.CTAinc.com

Unless otherwise indicated, Scripture quotations are from The Holy Bible, English Standard Version, copyright © 2001 by Crossway Bibles, a division of Good News Publishers. Used by permission. All rights reserved.

Scripture quotations marked (NIV®) are taken from the Holy Bible, New International Version®, NIV®. Copyright © 1973, 1978, 1984, 2011 by Biblica, Inc.™ Used by permission of Zondervan. All rights reserved worldwide. www.zondervan.com The "NIV" and "New International Version" are trademarks registered in the United States Patent and Trademark Office by Biblica, Inc.™

ISBN 978-1-943216-25-3
PRINTED IN THAILAND

RENEWED BY
CHRIST

Jesus said, "Come to me, all who labor and are heavy laden, and I will give you rest" (Matthew 11:28).

Jesus brings us rest. But he also brings renewal. The one who was there at creation, filling the world with life, continues to work creatively in our lives.

Let the readings and prayers this week lead you to Jesus, the source of renewal.

SCENES OF
RENEWAL

He who was seated on the throne said,
"Behold, I am making all things new!"
Revelation 21:5

I once bought a movie I will never watch again. Mel Gibson's *The Passion of the Christ*. The violence of that film was too graphic, the emotions too raw for me to ever watch it a second time.

I did view it once, however, and afterward there was a scene that played over and over in my head—the moment when Jesus speaks to his mother on the way to his crucifixion.

Jesus is carrying his cross. He is bloodied and beaten. He falls and Mary reaches out as if to catch him. She knows her son is going to die.

For a moment, we see the face of Jesus. Bruised and bloodied. And then we hear his voice. He says to Mary, "Behold, I make all things new."

In Jesus, this moment of horrible violence will be God's most creative act. By going to death, Jesus will bring forgiveness and life. He will rise from the dead and renew all things. For you.

This scene is not in the Gospels. Gibson made it up for the movie. But scenes like this occur throughout the Gospels. Again and again, we see Jesus enter suffering to bring about renewal.

Demon possession, leprosy, blindness, prostitution, poverty, death . . . the scenes change. But the work of Jesus remains the same. Jesus enters suffering to bring about renewal.

No wonder this scene played again and again in my head. This is the mission of Jesus, even today.

Have you seen suffering? A word spoken in anger that went too deep. An illness that medicine cannot cure. A memory of abuse that will not go away.

Turn your eyes to Jesus. He is the Lord of Life. He enters into suffering to bring about renewal and there is no road of suffering he will not travel, no place of pain he will not visit to bring renewal to you.

I don't know the road you walk. Yet, even in life's smallest scenes, Jesus walks with you. You are not alone.

Christ has come to renew your life, daily and richly, with the wonder of his love.

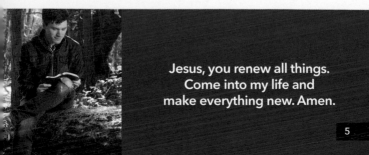

Jesus, you renew all things.
Come into my life and
make everything new. Amen.

LIFE-RENEWING
LOVE

But while he was still a long way off,
his father saw him and felt compassion,
and ran and embraced him and kissed him.

Luke 15:20

Who knew regret could be so heavy? For Greg, it go
heavier every year.

Five years ago, his dad died. A tragic accident on th
highway. But the accident wasn't as tragic as the years tha
led up to it. That's what kept Greg up at night.

He and his dad never really got along. Greg ha
intentionally fought with him over the years. Managin
money. Raising kids. The two were locked in an endles
battle of the wills.

The accident ended all of that. It ended the fighting. But
gave Greg an unending burden.

With his dad gone, there was no chance for reconciliation
Not even a simple "I'm sorry." So Greg lived with memorie
he could never change, words he could never say, and gui
that just wouldn't go away.

How do you bear the burden of a past you cannot change
Jesus offers an answer in the parable of the prodigal son.

he younger son left home with everything. And he turned with nothing. Nothing but regret. Words. Actions. ou name it. He had done it. Who knew regret could be so eavy? He had words he wanted to say. Words he thought ould make it better.

ut when his father saw him, he didn't wait for his son to peak. He ran and embraced him. His love had the first and e last word. In that moment, a lifetime of regret met an ernity of love. The father's love brought new life to an old ory of a lost son.

od's love is life renewing because it doesn't depend on hat we say or do but on what Jesus said and did for us. esus died under the tragedy of our sin so that he might se and create new life for us in himself.

e all carry burdens of regret. Words. Actions. You name We've done it. God's love, however, brings renewal out regret.

hen we face things we cannot change, God comes to fer us one thing that never changes. His love.

Father, forgive the things I cannot change. Receive and renew me with your unchanging love. Amen.

THE SMALLEST
DETAIL

He will wipe away every tear from their eyes.
Revelation 21:4

"Don't sweat the small stuff."

"Get the big picture."

"Go big or go home."

Proverbial sayings. Plastered on posters. Shared among friends. They ask us to take a larger look at life.

Sometimes, these sayings are helpful. They make you pause for a moment. Look up from your smartphone. See your family at breakfast . . . and "get the big picture." Answering e-mail is not really the point of vacation.

But, wise words can be misapplied. We can become so focused on the big picture that we lose sight of smaller things. We look to God to renew our lives. It's an astounding wonder! But then we overlook his powerful presence in the average day.

God once gave John a glorious vision of a new heaven and a new earth. The apostle saw multitudes of angels bowing in heavenly wonder. People from every tribe, language d nation gathering before God's throne. Yet, in the midst all of this magnificence, John sees God do the smallest ing. God wipes away a tear.

ie one who recreates the heavens and the earth takes ne to wipe away a tear.

hat God does in that one moment is itself a glorious velation. The kingdom of God comes in the smallest ways.

hrist once compared his death to a seed that was planted ohn 12:23–24). In the landscape of human history, the eath of one obscure Jewish man named Jesus was a small ing. Yet, in the kingdom of God, the largest of matters e decided in the smallest of ways.

y his death, Jesus brings forgiveness to all. He then es to rule over all creation. His rule, however, is often complished in the smallest of ways.

conversation with your daughter on the way home from hool fosters patience that lasts a lifetime. A prayer for ur marriage renews your relationship.

iese are small things, overlooked by a world that "goes g or goes home." But God, who takes time to wipe away tear, works through them.

the kingdom of God, small stuff matters . . . in a big way.

Almighty God, teach me to serve, trusting that the greatness of your kingdom comes in the smallest of ways. Amen.

RENEWAL IN
SUFFERING

Not only that, but we rejoice in our sufferings, knowing that suffering produces endurance.

Romans 5:3

At one point during the London Blitz, German fighters dropped almost 300 bombs per minute on the center of London. Such bombing destroyed more than the city's buildings. It reshaped people's lives.

Underground railway stations became places for shelter rather than transportation. Aboveground, life felt fragile as people walked to work through death, dust, and debris. People learned to see life differently.

Consider a photo from February 1942. It reveals a simple garden. In the center are carefully constructed plots. As you move outward, you come across landscaped mounds of earth. They form a circle around the garden. From even farther out, you see what this is. A victory garden planted in a bomb crater. From this scene of destruction come fruits of renewal.

The apostle Paul reminds us that renewal often comes in the midst of suffering. For this reason, Christians rejoice in their sufferings. We trust in God, who brings strength out of suffering. Renewal out of ruins.

When Christ died, he hung between men whose lives were ruins. We don't know what brought these criminals to crucifixion. It could have been a lifetime of stealing or simply one radically wrong decision. Regardless of what they did, they were done. A few hours more and they would breathe their last.

One criminal turned to Jesus. "Remember me when you come into your kingdom," he said (Luke 23:42). This dying man gave his ruined life to Jesus.

We don't know what brought this criminal to the cross, but we do know what brought Jesus there. An eternity of love and one radical, divine decision: Jesus would bring renewal out of ruins. He would die under sin's punishment to bring God's grace to sinners. And so he said to this man, "Today you will be with me in Paradise" (Luke 23:43).

Jesus brings life out of death. For this man and for you. There is no place in your life too ruined for him. No relationship so fractured, no memory so marred, no sin so great that Jesus can't bring renewal out of ruins.

Lord Jesus, I bring you the ruins of my life. Enter them and, by your Spirit, bring renewal. Amen.

A PLACE AT THE
TABLE

The Lord is not slow to fulfill his promise as some count slowness, but is patient toward you, not wishing that any should perish, but that all should reach repentance.

2 Peter 3:9

Your son used to look up to you. After soccer, he'd run to the car. The ride home was filled with talk about the game and questions about your opinion. That was only a year ago. Now it has all changed. Now, you're lucky if you're needed to pick him up. He usually tries to get a ride home with his friends. And, when you do pick him up, the ride home is awkward. Your apprehensive questions. His one-word answers. After a while, mutual silence settles in. He looks at his phone and you wonder where things went wrong.

Slowly, you learn that you can't control the love of your children.

You can, however, control your love for them. Peter reminds us that sometimes renewal takes time. "The Lord . . . is patient," he says (2 Peter 3:9). God doesn't work on our schedule. But he does work. He patiently waits . . . and loves.

Consider the night in the Upper Room before Jesus was arrested. Jesus knew that Judas was going to betray

m. Jesus could have excluded Judas. Turned the other sciples against him. Instead, Jesus chose to love. He knelt own like a servant and washed the feet of his betrayer. esus knew that renewal is possible only through love.

lthough Judas betrayed Jesus, Jesus wouldn't betray od's mission. He was patient. He died for sin and rose bring God's love to you. And not only to you, but also others through you.

o, what's a man to do when relationships change? ome retaliate in anger. Others walk away in regret. You, owever, are called to respond in love.

/hen a father realizes his children are growing distant, hat does he do? He goes to the kitchen and sets a place r them at the table. As long as he is the father and as ng as this is his household, there will always be a place the table for his children.

od's love is patient and strong. It waits and works enewal.

Lord, grant me patience to wait and strength to work as you renew relationships in your love. Amen.

FAITH WORKS

Throughout his earthly ministry, Jesus called people to come to him. He promised them rest and renewal for life. Unfortunately, not everyone responded to his call.

That problem continues today. Some people choose to go it alone.

Just because people won't come to Jesus, however, doesn't mean that he will not come to them.

This weekend, think about people you know who are trying to go it alone. If possible, give one or two of them a call. Send a text or an e-mail to see what's going on.

After you have connected, make a list of things you can pray about for them.

Take time to bring their names and their needs before Jesus. Then ask Jesus to work renewal in their lives.

RENEWED IN
BODY

One time during his ministry, Jesus sent his disciples out to work. When they returned, he called them to "come away by yourselves to a desolate place and rest a while" (Mark 6:31).

Jesus knew the importance of both labor and rest for his people. Without labor, our lives can seem pointless. Without rest, our bodies become exhausted.

By providing us both rest and labor, God renews our bodies.

Let the readings and prayers this week draw you closer to God so that, whether at rest or at work, you are renewed in body.

SABBATH
REST

[Jesus] said to them, "The Sabbath was made for man, not man for the Sabbath. So the Son of Man is lord even of the Sabbath."

Mark 2:27-28

He was flying . . . again.

His job had required twenty percent travel, but now averaged around fifty. "At least you still have a job his wife said, as he left for the airport. With layoffs ar restructuring, work was a mess. A hectic blessing.

As he looked out the airplane window, he saw fields le unplanted. Dark patches of earth in a landscape of greei Fallow ground. The ancient art of crop rotation is still bein practiced today.

Before the advent of industrialized agriculture, farme relied upon crop rotation to restore the nutrient balance the soil. Leaving a section of land unplanted for a seaso helped restore the health of the soil.

As with land, so with those who live on it. Rest provide renewal.

When God prepared his people for life in the Promise Land, he gave them the Sabbath. One day a week, ther would be rest. Why?

od gave two reasons. creation and redemption. In xodus, the Sabbath was connected to creation. God sted after his good work creating the world (Exodus 0:11). In Deuteronomy, the Sabbath was connected redemption. God's people rested, after he graciously elivered them from slavery (Deuteronomy 5:15). God's oodness and grace gave shape to life.

od's kingdom has a rhythm of remembrance, rest, nd renewal.

nfortunately, Sabbath rest is sometimes distant from ur lives. Daily business distracts us. With deadlines and emands, product quotas and performance reviews, we nmerse ourselves in our work for others and overlook od's good and gracious work for us.

od sent Jesus to be your Lord of the Sabbath. In him, od's goodness and grace are present for you. By his eath, Jesus graciously delivers you from sin. By his esurrection, he lives to work good for you.

ake this moment to see that small patch of land. Don't just ee it from a distance. Come and live in it. Experience rest nat renews.

esus is your Lord of the Sabbath. His work provides rest nat renews for life.

Jesus, Lord of the Sabbath, lead
me to rest in your good and
gracious work that I might
be renewed. Amen.

FED AND
NOURISHED

But they urged him strongly, saying "Stay with us,
for it is toward evening and the day is now far spent."
Luke 24:29

Homes used to have formal living rooms. As a frien[d]
explained, "That was the room you never went into. It wa[s]
reserved for guests."

Now, with open-concept floor plans, the formal living roo[m]
is gone. It died from lack of use.

One wonders if kitchens might experience a similar fate.

"Do you want breakfast?"

"No, I'll just pick something up on the way to work."

"Are you coming home for dinner?"

"No, I'll grab something after school and stay fo[r]
the game."

Removing kitchens from homes would never happe[n]
but we have begun to remove home-cooked meals fro[m]
our lives.

ast food and faster lives have made for more eating on the
o and less eating at home. Less cooking. Less community.
ess conversation . . . in the place we call home.

ow strange that, after his resurrection, Jesus revealed
mself at meals. Cooking fish on the shore for his disciples.
ating dinner with the disciples on the road to Emmaus.

ne would think that Jesus had better things to do. He
ad defeated sin and death. He had risen to rule over all
ings. Yet, Jesus took time for a meal. Cooking, eating,
onversing. In these things, Jesus worked renewal.

was late and they were tired from the journey. But the
mmaus disciples invited their traveling companion in.
s they ate, they saw Jesus. Their Savior from sin sat with
em at table, and they were renewed.

esus began his ministry alone, fasting forty days in the
esert. He would not end it that way. Why? Because he died
o remove the sin that separates us from God and he rose
o give us his Spirit that unites and renews. Descriptions of
s future kingdom are filled with feasts and banquets and,
ntil then, Jesus will be present at ordinary meals.

Vith Jesus, renewal can happen in something as simple
s a meal.

ake time to consider the people you interact with today.
Vhy has God brought you together? How is God at work
this place?

Be with us, Jesus, in something as
simple as a meal. Grant us your food
that nourishes and your Spirit that
renews. Amen.

THE GIVER OF
LIFE

These all look to you, to give them their food in due season
Psalm 104:27

Baby-proofing your house. That's what they call it. Cabinet are fastened. Sharp corners covered. Anything that coul (but shouldn't) get kicked, thrown, or eaten is removed Baby-proofing creates a safe place for your children.

In addition to baby-proofing, however, there is also "baby planning." Parents create a world for their children t discover. They "baby plan" their homes.

On the bedroom wall, animals peek out from behin letters. Your child grows and discovers G and giraffe. H begins to name the world. The fridge is a mess of littl creamed creations. Why? Because you are giving you daughter different foods. Inspiring her taste buds. Rockin her little world.

Baby-planning brings discovery, and discovery bring delight in the basic wonders of the world.

Too bad someone can't "adult plan" our world.

So often we get caught up in the routine. We hear, see, an do what we need to get by. The world around us shrink

nd our lives shrink with it. Immersed in routine, we need
o be renewed.

salm 104 sings a song of renewal. It awakens us. Opens
ur eyes to see the wonder of God's creation. God's world
 too amazing, too great for us to discover completely.
What we do see, however, renews our reliance on God.

his God, who created all life, cares for his creatures. He
ade his care known most fully in Jesus. In Jesus, the God
ho gave you life literally gave his life for you. He died and
se to reveal God's love and renew your reliance on him.

ou go for a run, along a trail you always take, listening
 a playlist you always play. You don't see the world as it
ally is.

ut, then, it hits you. The smell of grass. Freshly mown.
weet with summer. For a moment, you take out your
arbuds and discover God's world.

et that moment of wonder renew your reliance on God.
sten to his playlist. Sing his song of creation. Remember
e Giver of life, who gave his life for you.

Almighty God, you create and
sustain all things. Awaken me
to the wonder of your world
and renew my reliance on you.
Amen.

JOYFUL
WORK

The LORD God took the man and put him in the Garden of Eden to work it and keep it.

Genesis 2:15

"Just trying to make it to Friday," Bill said. Outside hi cubicle, co-workers laughed. It was Monday . . . and h was already looking forward to Friday.

Isn't that how it goes? Sometimes, we just need to ge through the week. "Life is more than work," we say, an we separate ourselves from our jobs. Work become something we just need to get through.

There's a reason for that. After disobeying God, Adam an Eve experienced his judgment. God said, "By the swea of your face you shall eat bread" (Genesis 3:19). For thi reason, labor is hard.

Exhausting.

But there is another picture of labor in Scripture. A vision where work is not something we get through, bu something we give through.

When God first made the world, he placed Adam and Ev in the Garden of Eden. He gave them work to do. Wor was not a result of sin. It was actually part of God's plan. A blessing from God.

God obviously didn't need human labor. After all, he had just created the world. Why, then, did he put Adam and Eve to work?

Because God wanted to share his joy in working. Adam and Eve would make something and see that it was good. They would give through work and discover joy in a job well done.

Consider how God gives through his work. Taking the dust of the ground into his hands, God breathes and gives us life. Taking the sins of the world upon his back, Jesus dies and gives new life. Life that is renewed in the joy of work.

During his ministry, Jesus renewed people for work. Consider Zacchaeus. He was a tax collector in Jericho. Making a living by taking from others. After meeting Jesus, however, his life was changed. Beginning that day, the world was a place where he showed God's grace by giving to others.

Forgiveness renews us for labor. God invites us to enjoy his world by working in it. Making a living by giving through work.

Jesus, teach us to give through the work that we do and renew our joy in a job well done. Amen.

A LABOR OF
LOVE

*If anyone serves, they should do so with
the strength God provides.*
1 Peter 4:11 NIV®

"Dad, can you open this?" Marissa handed him the jar
Pretending to sweat and to strain because of the challenge
José quickly took off the lid.

Men are often associated with strength. Whether it's lifting
weights or moving furniture, we master challenges with
brute power and force.

Sometimes, however, life presents a different kind o
challenge that calls for a different kind of strength.

His son was struggling at school. He'd come home angry
and ready to pick a fight. Now was not the time for powe
but patience. Not force but finesse.

Not all jobs are feats of strength. Some are a labor of love

Consider the ministry of Jesus. When surrounded by
soldiers in the Garden of Gethsemane, Jesus did not pick
up a sword to fight. Instead, he patiently suffered betrayal
trial, and crucifixion. He suffered in order to save.

esus made the power of his love known in weakness. Once urrounded by angels, he set aside his heavenly throne nd hung among criminals. The author of life experienced leath. For you. This was his labor of love.

By bearing God's eternal wrath, Jesus brings you God's eternal love. His love has power to renew.

Look at your life. Are there problems too complex for a imple show of strength? relationships you no longer know now to handle? Consider the labor of love.

Laboring with God's love is mysterious. Love is powerful because it comes as a servant. Mastery occurs in ministry.

Consider sports. You don't master a golf swing by force but inesse. You know the game so well and enter into it so fully hat you can feel a good swing in your bones. The same is rue with our Lord's love.

A child's dashed hopes, a broken promise, a strained elationship, these things are not overcome overnight. One cannot will them away. Instead one works with the trength that God offers. A love that is patient. A heart that s open. A word that is kind.

Problems may not disappear, but Christ will be present, enewing you to live and to labor in love.

Savior of sinners, you are the strength of your people. Let your saving love shape our service. Amen.

FAITH WORKS

In Acts, the early church collected food and distributed it to those in need. God's people knew that Jesus cared for others through their acts of service, even attending to bodily needs.

Take time this weekend to put together a donation to a local charity, a food pantry, or a homeless shelter.

Identify the charity and call to see if there is anything that is needed. Do they have any restrictions on what might be donated?

Then, collect materials to offer to others. Put together a personal care kit for the homeless. Donate canned food to a pantry, blankets to a shelter.

Take time to make a difference. When you have lost everything, even the smallest of items are considered a blessing. That someone saw you in need and responded in love gives hope for renewal.

RENEWED IN
MIND

Throughout his ministry, Jesus teaches. Not just in the synagogues, but out in the world.

In a house in Capernaum, on the shores of Galilee, up on a mountainside, Jesus gathered crowds to himself and taught.

Jesus continues to teach today through the Scriptures. He renews our minds so that we trust in him and see God at work in the world.

Let the readings and prayers this week open the Scriptures, so that you are renewed in mind.

GOD'S GREATER
STORY

*Do not be conformed to this world, but be
transformed by the renewal of your mind.*

Romans 12:2

"Don't give me any of your Christian stuff," she said. "As
far as I'm concerned, your religion is hate speech."

Jeff was shocked at Gretchen's anger. A recent bombing
brought up religious extremism. When he tried to bring up
his faith, Gretchen wouldn't have it.

She knew about Christianity. It was a story of sin and
punishment. She wanted nothing to do with Jeff's angry
God. As far as she was concerned, an angry God bred
angry people, always accusing others of sin. "Of course
there are mass shootings," she said, "with a God like that."

Unfortunately, Gretchen isn't the only one confused.
Sometimes God's people get confused as well. Their story
of God is too small.

Consider the disciples. They see a blind man begging and
say to Jesus, "Rabbi, who sinned, this man or his parents,
that he was born blind?" (John 9:2).

See how small their story is? It begins with sin ("Rabbi, who
sinned") and ends with punishment ("that he was born

blind"). They stand apart from the world and talk about people rather than live in the world and work for God.

Jesus, however, knows God's greater story. It doesn't begin with sin but creation. It doesn't end with punishment but restoration. When your story begins with creation and ends with restoration, every moment in between is a time when God brings life.

So Jesus says to his disciples, "It was not that this man sinned, or his parents, but that the works of God might be displayed in him" (John 9:3).

God's work is to renew all things. God created the world and, in Jesus, he will restore it. By his death, Jesus repairs creation. By his rising, he promises restoration.

So rather than stand there and talk theology, Jesus kneels down and lives it. He heals this man. He also heals you.

Jesus will not let your life be determined by your sin. He brings you into God's greater story and transforms your life with his love.

Live, then, not by the littleness of your mind, but by the greatness of God's kingdom.

Jesus, send your Spirit to display
the works of God in my life. Amen.

A GREATER VISION

*But they who wait for the LORD shall renew their
strength; they shall mount up with wings like eagles.*

Isaiah 40:31

The evening is quiet. Just the wind, a few birds, and casua
conversation on the porch. Suddenly Skippy's ears perk up
He listens intently.

Conversation stops, everyone looks around, and Curt says
"He hears something." Then they start talking again.

Strange how an animal can awaken us to a world we do
not know. Dogs hear at a frequency beyond that which is
detectable by humans. Their sense of smell astounds us
even more. Researchers say that a dog can smell one gram
of sweat in a 135-square-mile area.

Imagine the world a dog senses as you open the door
No wonder they invite us to respond with caution or to
bound with excitement as we make our way into the world
Perhaps God has surrounded us with animals to awaken us
to a world we do not know.

Certainly God did that with the Scriptures. God spoke to
his people through the prophets.

The prophets were tuned by the Spirit to hear what we could not hear and to see what we could not see. When they opened their mouths, God opened people's eyes to see his work in the world. This vision renews our hope.

Isaiah offers a word to God's people at a time when even the stronghearted were weary. Israel was in exile. They were without king, without kingdom, without temple, without priest, without worship, without sacrifice. But they were never without God. Through his Word, God promised them an unconquerable love.

That promise was fulfilled in Jesus Christ. God came into our world to deliver us from captivity to sin and evil. By dying and rising, Jesus revealed a love beyond our imagination. A caring that cannot be conquered.

We cannot plan our future, and sometimes that leads to fear. A father lies awake at night, thinking about his daughter. Will she be okay when he is gone? He looks and listens intently.

God's love conquers such fear.

The future, unknown to us, is already known to God and nothing can destroy God's future plans for you.

Lord, help me to trust in your ways, ways beyond my understanding, that I might live in hope. Amen.

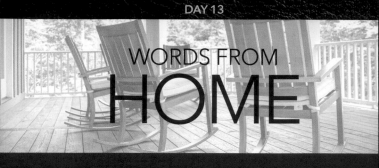

WORDS FROM
HOME

As far as the east is from the west, so far does he remove our transgressions from us.

Psalm 103:12

They found the dorm, met her roommate, unpacked the car, and moved all of her stuff into the room. Even the overstuffed box that everyone told her was too heavy to carry. Now, there was nothing left to do but say good-bye. The heaviest burden of all.

He hugged her and said, "I love you. Have fun. Remember, you're still my little girl." As he walked away, he thought how stupid that sounded. But that's how he felt.

When you have the whole world before you, it's easy to get lost. He wanted to give her something—a word from home—to remember that she was loved.

Before Israel entered the Promised Land, God spoke to them through Moses. In the midst of all of God's commandments for life and all of God's promises for care, God gave them one simple direction. He asked that his words be read in the presence of the people every seven years (Deuteronomy 31:10–11).

ery seven years, God's people would gather to hear these rds from God. They would remember God's mighty eds. How he delivered them from Egypt, sustained em through the wilderness, and brought them into this omised Land.

ese were words from home. They would know that he as their God and that they were his people, his children roughout all generations.

or Christians, the world can be a difficult place. Tests and mptations. Sin, sex, and suffering. It's easy to fall and to el far from God. The psalmist, however, wants us to know at we are always God's children. For this reason, he offers words from home.

far as the east is from the west, so far has God removed ur transgressions from us. There is no place where you are eyond the love of God.

/hen Christ died on the cross, he stretched his arms out ide. He took upon himself all your sin for all time. In doing at, he opened the world for you.

here is no place you can go where you are not his child. orgiven and loved.

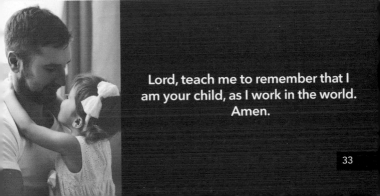

Lord, teach me to remember that I
am your child, as I work in the world.
Amen.

TRUTH IN
LOVE

*Rather, speaking the truth in love, we are to grow up in
every way into him who is the head, into Christ.*

Ephesians 4:15

Fishing had suddenly become more personal. Dan brough
up the topic of his daughter. Last month, she told th
family she was gay. Carlos didn't know how to respond
This conversation wasn't one he wanted to have. He kne
God's Word but he didn't know how to say it. This wasn't
hypothetical situation.

This was Dan, his friend. Asking real questions. About
real daughter. To a real friend.

As our culture changes, Christians are faced with difficu
questions. People ask us, "What does your church sa
about . . .?" and you can fill in the blank. Gay marriage
Science. War. Abortion. Other religions. The topics chang
over time.

What doesn't change, however, is God's call to Christian
to "give an answer to everyone who asks you to give th
reason for the hope that you have" (1 Peter 3:15 NIV®).

As Christians, it's easy to isolate ourselves from suc
conversations or to provide quick answers. The Bible i

uickly quoted and the conversation ends in arguments
nd in anger.

ut, when the questions are personal, so is God's answer.
is answer is clear, but it's also personal.

aravaggio once painted a picture of Jesus with doubting
homas. Thomas stands there with his questions and
esus answers them. Personally. He takes Thomas' hand
nd guides his finger into his side. No questions threaten
esus. He takes time to answer them. Personally and
ith love.

/hen the world was lost in sin, God did not send a book
f answers. He sent a person. His Son. Jesus. Jesus lived,
ied, and rose again to forgive all sin, to save all people,
nd to change all lives through a relationship with him.

or personal questions, we have a personal Savior who
kes time to draw us deeper into a relationship with
imself. All questions, then, are opportunities for Jesus to
art a personal relationship with people.

or our world's many questions, we have more than a book
f answers. We have Jesus, who takes people by the hand
nd speaks the truth in love.

Savior, you made yourself known
to those who struggle. Help me
bring those who have questions
into a deeper relationship with you.
Amen.

REMEMBERING
GRACE

I will remember the deeds of the LORD.
Psalm 77:11

Consider the power of memory.

Tim stands there after his father's funeral, greeting people A friend mentions his dad's humor and they remembe a few jokes. And how stupid they were. For a momen shoulders relax and weary faces brighten, even at a funera

Why? Because memory has the power to take us awa from the present.

It can also do something more powerful still.

Memory can bring us more fully into the present.

Your parents have come to the hospital. It's the first tim your mom gets to hold her new grandson. At first, she i nervous. It's been so long since she held a baby. But the she talks about how she held you and rocked you to slee She remembers. You watch as she begins to rock him. Sh leans down and kisses his forehead.

This time, memory doesn't take someone away from th present. No. It brings her more fully into it.

The psalmist says, "I will remember the deeds of the LORD." Why? What happens when we remember?

Some would argue that remembering God takes you away from the present. It hinders rather than helps.

Life has changed since the Scriptures were written. If you remember God, they say, you will be odd. Out of sync with the world. You don't get ahead at work by "turning the other cheek," and you won't enjoy the good life at home if you constantly care for the poor.

But what if the God you remember created the world? What if he holds the past, the present, and the future in his hands?

If this is the God you remember, then remembering brings you more fully to life. Because life itself is God's gift to you.

Before you were born, God knew you. Before the world was created, he chose you. Jesus died to end the power of sin and he rose to bring new life to all people.

Because Jesus is the author of life, every day has eternal meaning. Remembering him, you are drawn into the world, for works that truly matter and a love that outlives all time.

Gracious God, help me remember your work in the past that I might live in the present with assurance of your love. Amen.

FAITH WORKS

The apostle Paul encourages the Christians in Rome to set their minds not on the flesh but on the Spirit, because "to set the mind on the Spirit is life and peace" (Romans 8:6).

One way to set your mind on the Spirit is to choose a passage from Scripture and live with it for a while.

Choose a passage from Scripture, perhaps one used in the devotions this past week. Write it out on a small piece of paper. Then put that paper in your pocket or wallet and carry it around with you during the day.

At different times, read and reflect on the passage. How does it bring you encouragement? How can it shape your life or your response to the world?

Discover how God uses the mind set on the Spirit to bring life and peace.

RENEWED IN
SPIRIT

During his ministry, Jesus frequently tells people to "take heart."

Whether it is a paralytic who lies before him, a sick woman, or frightened disciples, Jesus has a way of renewing the spirit.

Sometimes the burdens we carry are not seen by others. They are buried deep within the heart.

Jesus, who rules all things, has both the power and the desire to renew your heart, your spirit.

Let the readings and prayers this week draw you closer to Jesus, so that you are renewed in spirit.

THE HEART OF THE
MATTER

*Create in me a clean heart, O God,
and renew a right spirit within me.*
Psalm 51:10

Sarah looked out the window and saw her husband cleaning the deck. She smiled.

They had had another argument. About the kids. Instead of apologizing, Bill changed his clothes and started working.

Other women might be upset. But Sarah knew Bill. She had been asking him for weeks to clean the deck for their son's graduation. Now, she saw his apology. She thought, "His heart is in the right place."

Outward actions are important in life. But more important still is the inner life of the heart. When your heart is in the right place, everything else will follow.

Unfortunately, King David learned this the hard way. He had followed the sexual desires of his heart. He took another man's wife, and now he was battling to maintain outward appearances.

He had the husband killed. He took the widow into his palace. Outwardly, he ruled the kingdom. But inwardly adultery, deceit, and murder ruled his heart.

o one knew. Except the Lord. For God knows the desires
f the heart.

od sent Nathan to confront David and David confessed
s sin. But he also offered this powerful prayer. "Create in
e a pure heart, O God."

avid had learned the heart of the matter. When your heart
in the right place, the rest will follow. This king no longer
ught to rule an outward kingdom. He called for God to
ome and rule his heart.

ecause of sin, our hearts are broken. We are not right with
od. But broken hearts break the heart of God. For that
eason, God sent his Son, Jesus. He came not to seek an
utward kingdom but to rule our hearts.

t his death, Jesus won your greatest battle. He took your
n, the sin that separates you from God and gave you his
ghteousness to renew your life with God.

hrough faith, Christ rules your heart and renews your life.

ife is filled with many battles. Sometimes you don't know
here to begin. God takes you to the heart of the matter—
is love for you.

When God rules your heart, the rest of life will follow.

Create in me a clean heart,
O God, that in my life I
follow you. Amen.

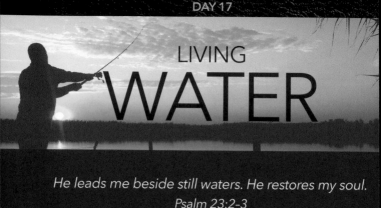

LIVING
WATER

He leads me beside still waters. He restores my soul.
Psalm 23:2-3

Jesus and his disciples are passing through Samaria. The stop at a town called Sychar. The disciples go into town t get food to care for their bodies. But Jesus stays behind outside at a well, to care for someone's soul.

She came to the well to draw water. This woman. It was no a moment of rest and relaxation. It was work. Hard work.

Hard work made harder by the burdens she carried. Th men she had known. So marked was she by all of he marriages, that the man she was now with would not eve give her the honor of being called his wife. He was just on more man in a line of men, leading her to feel less human Less loved. A lost soul.

She came to the well to draw water but what she needed was someone who could restore her soul.

How do you restore a soul? The body can be healed. A surgeon can cut your flesh, open your chest, and reach in and actually touch your beating heart.

...ut your soul. That's a different matter.

...can't be seen or touched by human hands. Yet it feels
...e touch of life. Abuse that ends a childhood too early.
...miscarriage that ends fatherhood. A lie that fractures
...marriage.

...hese things cut deeper than any surgeon's knife. They
...ouch your soul. Making it restless. Longing for restoration.
...or the life that only God can give.

...o this one woman at this one well is not the only one who
...broken. In need of restoration. Yet, to her, to you, the
...avior comes.

...conversation, Jesus offers her water. Living water. But, it
...oesn't come from any well. It comes from him. God's love
...ows into the world in Jesus. His death for our sin is God's
...ift of life. His love is a life-giving stream. Jesus comes and
...estores this woman. He makes her a child of God.

...e still comes. This Jesus. Our shepherd. Out to the lonely
...laces of broken bodies and lost souls. He brings us his
...tream of living water. Grace that saves. Love that renews.

**O Lord, my Shepherd,
provide your living water to
restore my soul. Amen.**

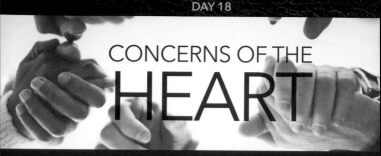

CONCERNS OF THE
HEART

*We do not know what to pray for as we ought, but the Spir(it)
himself intercedes for us with groanings too deep for word(s).*
Romans 8:26

Sometimes an imaginary story can lead us to the truth.

Consider the old preacher's tale. Abraham and Isaac talking
after a long night.

Isaac had gone out and had never come home. Searching
for lost sheep, he got lost himself. He spent the night i(n)
the wilderness. The next day, when Abraham found him(,)
he was pretty bad off. Scared. Alone.

"Why didn't you pray?" Abraham asked. "You might have
felt lost, but you weren't lost to God. God could still hea(r)
your prayers."

"I didn't know what to say," he said.

"What about all of those prayers we taught you? Wh(y)
didn't you pray one of them?"

"I couldn't remember them," Isaac stammered. After (a)
pause, he added, "Dad, I was scared."

"Were you so scared that you forgot your alphabet?"
Abraham asked.

No," Isaac said. "I remember the alphabet. *Aleph, beth, gimel . . .*"

Then why didn't you pray the alphabet?" Abraham asked.

Isaac laughed. "What do you mean? Just say the alphabet? That's not a prayer."

Sometimes," Abraham said, "when you don't know what to pray, you just give God the letters and he'll make them into words."

This imaginary story proclaims a real truth. God is able to take the concerns of your heart and turn them into prayer.

Life gets complicated. Mistakes make our lives a mess. We want to pray but don't know how. We can't begin to put it all into words.

On the cross, Christ took our sin and punishment. He stretched out his arms to gather all the burnt-out ends of our broken days. He is the Alpha and Omega. The Word of God for you. Your ends are his beginning. He rose from death and brings about renewal of life. For you.

When we've reached the end and don't know what to say, the apostle Paul gives us this encouragement. "The Spirit . . . intercedes for us with groanings too deep for words."

When you are at the end of words, by God's grace, the Spirit speaks for you.

Holy Spirit, take the concerns
of my heart and put them into
words to work wonders
for my soul. Amen.

45

A GUARDED
HEART

And the peace of God, which surpasses all understanding
will guard your hearts and your minds in Christ Jesus.
Philippians 4:7

Guarded. That's what he was.

His daughter was sick and he was doing all that he could to protect her. He had taken off work. Spent hours at the hospital. The doctors finally determined it was juvenile diabetes.

Until that time, however, it was touch and go. He didn't want to lose her. He had lost his marriage. He wouldn't lose his little girl.

He hadn't called the church to inform them. He didn't want to see the pastor. He was angry at God. Then, that morning, he saw the refrigerator magnet as he walked out the door.

The youth minister had distributed these magnets. A picture of Jesus, with his arms wide open, holding a young man, welcoming him home.

His daughter loved that magnet. She put it on the fridge.

he minister had talked about images of God. Pictures that
e carry around in our minds. He contrasted this picture of
esus with a Far Side cartoon.

the cartoon, God was sitting at a computer looking at the
creen. He was watching a man walking along the sidewalk
ith a piano suspended in the air above his head. God had
is finger hovering over a key on the keyboard. The key
ead "smite." God was about to hit the smite button.

Which God comes to mind when something bad
appens?" the youth minister asked. "A God who is sitting
here, planning to smite you, or a God who is holding on
o you, welcoming you home?"

esus came to give you a true picture of God. God so
oved the world that he sent his Son to bear your sin and
o be your Savior. This Jesus comes to strengthen you. To
upport you. To be there to welcome you home.

eeing that refrigerator magnet changed things. God
pened the man's heart to the presence of Christ.

he man had guarded his daughter and guarded his heart
ut the true protector was Jesus, sending his Spirit to
eassure him of God's love and God's work in the midst
f trial.

Jesus, grant me courage in time
of trial. Draw me closer to you,
through your Spirit, who guards
my heart with your powerful love.
Amen.

RENEWED BY
LOVE

A new commandment I give to you, that you love one another: just as I have loved you, you also are to love one another. By this all people will know that you are my disciples, if you have love for one another.

John 13:34–35

They were watching *The King's Speech*, when Andrew shifted and rolled onto the remote. The screen froze, which only made the king's problem worse.

As the drama stopped on the screen, mundane activity started in the room. People were getting up, turning on lights, looking for the remote. In the midst of all this commotion, something strange happened. Someone started looking at the screen. Commenting on it so others would see.

When the movie wasn't moving forward, small details became more important. The characters' costumes. The way the light came in through the window. Instead of watching a movie, waiting to see what would happen, people were meditating on a moment. Allowing it to sink in.

Something similar happens in John's Gospel. The passion of Jesus is filled with action. Passover, Gethsemane, the religious leaders, Pilate, Herod, the soldiers, the cross. So much happens in so little time, that it is easy to get lost in the action.

esus, however, pauses for a moment. He offers his disciples a moment to remember. To meditate on and to live in.

esus has just done the task of a servant. He has washed is disciples' feet. Before they proceed with the Passover, lowever, Jesus asks his disciples to meditate on what his means.

"A new command I give you," Jesus says, "Love one nother."

t was old—this command to love. But it was also new— n him.

That night the disciples would see a love beyond their understanding. Jesus would offer his life to forgive their sins.

Jesus knew the wonder of this love. His forgiveness would enew their spirits. His love would change how their lives had meaning in him.

The smallest task, like washing feet, would be a way of showing the deepest love.

Discipleship is not always filled with powerful moments, worthy of the big screen. Sometimes, it's the smallest things—watching your kid play soccer—that reveal the greatest love.

Lord, your love fills the mundane
with heavenly meaning.
Empower me to serve
in humble but holy ways. Amen.

FAITH WORKS

In Psalm 42, we hear the prayer of the downcast. Someone lonely and abandoned cries out to God. In the midst of that prayer, however, this person remembers what it was like to worship with God's people. That memory brings comfort. A connection. Hope.

Hospitals and nursing homes are places where people often feel downcast or alone. Recovering from sickness or living with illness can be a long journey. Yet God cares for such people, renewing their spirits.

Take time today to put together a care package for someone in need. Call a local nursing home or hospital and ask if there is anything you can bring.

Gather the items together, include a short note promising your prayers, and drop the package off to be shared with someone in need.

Trust that God works through your actions as you offer him your prayers.

RENEWED FOR
LIFE

After his resurrection, Jesus appeared to his disciples and renewed their faith. He encouraged them and strengthened them and then sent them out into the world.

Jesus continues this work today. With you. Jesus renews your body, mind, and spirit, that you might find life in him and be part of his work in the world.

Let the readings and prayers this week draw you closer to Jesus, so that you are renewed for life.

THE SPIRIT OF
LIFE

Exalted at the right hand of God, and having received from the Father the promise of the Holy Spirit, he has poured out this that you yourselves are seeing and hearing.

Acts 2:33

In the German film *Wings of Desire*, there's a scene where angels pass through a library.

At first, you are in the presence of angels. Hovering high above a reading room. Below you are rows of tables. People sit close to one another but remain separate. Reading and writing in their own little worlds.

Then, the angels descend and pass through the library. As they come near the people, you hear the voices of these people silently reading.

Walking with angels brings you closer to people. For a moment, you hear what is on their minds.

In some ways, that scene is a picture of how God works in the world. Jesus came to end the separation between sinners and God. His death opened the kingdom of heaven to us. And his Spirit creates a community of people who live in God's love.

When Jesus ascended, he told his disciples to remain in Jerusalem until they were "clothed with power from on high" (Luke 24:49).

This power of Jesus, however, was unlike anything the disciples had ever seen. It was not the power of wealth or warriors. It was the power of his Spirit working through his Word.

On Pentecost, his Word brought life. A few words from a few disciples touched hearts, opened minds, and added thousands to the church. While the Romans governed with armies, God ruled the world through his Word.

Jesus sent his Spirit to bring life, and he still sends that Spirit today.

Look around you. See how people sit with one another in common places but don't interact. Instead, they look intently at their phones. This is what our world calls being connected.

Jesus creates a different kind of connection. He works through you. Creating community, not just online but in person. Life in the Spirit from the Spirit of life.

Take time to be present with someone around you today. With the presence of Jesus and the power of his Spirit, a simple conversation can make a connection and lead to a deeper spiritual life.

Holy Spirit, open my life to your presence and my world to your work. Amen.

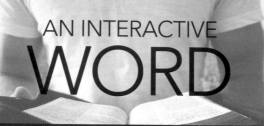

AN INTERACTIVE
WORD

Taste and see that the LORD is good!
Psalm 34:8

Brian was in the family room with the kids, when he turned on the TV to catch the end of the game. Carly, his youngest walked over to the screen. She reached up and swiped it with her hand. Nothing happened. So, she tapped it and then swiped again.

Carly had grown up with a touch screen and not a remote. She expected communication to be interactive. Rather than sit on the couch and flip through the channels, she wanted to touch and swipe and select what she would do on the screen.

Isn't that how God encourages us to read his Word? Interactively.

The psalmist asks us to taste the Word of God and experience its goodness. James encourages us to do more than listen. "Do not merely listen to the word, and so deceive yourselves. Do what it says" (James 1:22 NIV®)

When God made his saving love known to the world, he did not just put it on a banner in the sky. No. God came into the world in Jesus Christ. He took on flesh. He became human.

esus interacted with our sin, suffering its punishment, o that we might interact with God's grace, experiencing :s wonder.

A city church once saw what this was like. The reading for Sunday was the parable of Lazarus and the rich man (Luke 6:19–31). In the parable, extraordinary poverty lay at the door of extraordinary wealth.

n preparation for that reading, the minister invited members to take pictures of the poverty they passed by during the week. That Sunday, they saw picture after picture of the needs of their city. Lazarus was still there, lying by the doors of the wealthy, waiting for the work of God.

Those pictures became invitations for those members to put faith into practice. In each picture, God was calling them to care for the poor. God's people became more active in the city. They wouldn't overcome the problems of poverty, but they would reveal God's presence lovingly active among his people.

God's love for you is interactive. Changing your life and, through your life, changing the world.

Almighty and ever-living God, teach me to taste and see that you are good. Renew my life with your interactive Word. Amen.

THE POWER OF
GOD

So then, death is at work in us, but life is at work in you.
2 Corinthians 4:12 NIV®

The apostle Paul compared his life to a jar of clay. Weak. Easily broken.

But, Paul knew the power of God. He would never be beaten. Never cast aside by God. God was able to work in weakness.

So often people assume that God is only found among the strong. Goliath laughed at the shepherd David. The religious leaders demanded that Jesus come down from the cross. People look for God in places of strength.

Where people see weakness, they don't see God.

"I don't have any of those skills," he says, when asked about going on a medical mission trip. "I first need to get things sorted out at home," his friend says, when asked about church.

Seeing our weaknesses, our sins, we stand at a distance. We work and we wait for things to get better. We think, "God can only work if I've got it all together."

We really need to listen to Paul.

Paul knew that God works in weakness. He had seen it in his own life. When persecuted, he was not abandoned. When struck down, he was not destroyed. If God could take someone who actively persecuted Christians, forgive him, and use him to build his Church, then God could work with anyone with any weakness.

He could and he does.

Jesus died to forgive your sins but he also rose to work in your life. This one who fought and overcame death has the power to work through your weakness and bring his grace to the world. When you are weak, he is strong.

Al was undergoing radiation. It was an outpatient procedure. Every week, for six weeks, he would lie still while the therapist positioned and operated the machine.

During this time, Al decided to pray. Not for himself but for others. He asked the therapist if there was anything for which she'd like him to pray. "My family," she said. "Things are not good at home."

That small offer of prayer began a new life for her. A return to discipleship. In the midst of weakness, God was at work.

Almighty God, may your power to work in weakness open my life to your ways in the world. Amen.

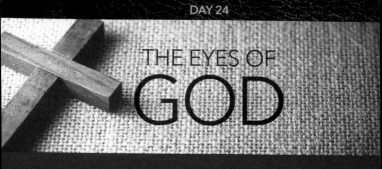

THE EYES OF
GOD

*Restore to me the joy of your salvation and grant
me a willing spirit, to sustain me.*
Psalm 51:12 NIV®

Have you, like the psalmist, ever prayed for a willing spirit
to sustain you?

Sometimes, life in God's kingdom loses its luster. The daily
joy of God's salvation becomes the daily grind of work in
the world.

When he first became a father, Brad approached that
work with wonder. Caring for his daughter was something
beautiful and important, something God had entrusted to
him.

Then, slowly, the wonder faded. Being a dad no longer
seemed holy. It was just routine. Helping Eva eat. Listening
to why she didn't want to wear those shoes. He was still
doing the work of God, being a father, but he no longer
lived in the wonder of God's work.

The prayer goes up for a willing spirit. Can God restore
the joy?

Consider Emil. When he first started teaching, Emil hung a
painting in his office. A white lamb on a black background.

he title was *Good Friday*. The painting reminded him of e joy of his salvation.

od sent his Son, Jesus, to be the sacrificial lamb to take way our sins.

ver time, however, it became just a painting. Something e no longer saw, hanging on the wall.

ne day, during a student consultation, God restored the y. The student was sharing his struggles. Not just in school ut at home. As they talked, Emil glanced up. Behind the udent was that painting. The certainty of God's love.

uddenly, Emil saw things with the eyes of God. This tudent was someone Jesus died for and this conversation as part of God's work in his life. Daily routine became a me for divine discipleship.

/e all need a painting like that, hovering in the background, > help us see God at work in our daily lives. That way we ill know what we are really doing, whether we are at the ffice or on the sidelines of the soccer field. We are serving eople for whom Christ died.

he joy of salvation comes when we see life with the eyes f God.

Lord, restore to me the joy of your salvation. Open my eyes and help me to see your will in my daily work. Amen.

THE HANDS OF
GOD

[Jesus said,] "Follow me, and I will make you fishers of men"
Matthew 4:19

If you were to go to the city of Florence and stand in th[e] hallway of the *Gallerie dell'Accademia*, you'd find yourse[lf] surrounded by sculptures. Masterfully incomplete.

Four pieces of unfinished stone stand before you. A[n] artist was working on marble but stopped in the middle o[f] his work.

The edges are rough. The figures are incomplete. And, ye[t] you can see the beginning of something beautiful.

It looks like people are emerging from these rocks. Som[e] have no faces. Others lack arms. These are merely th[e] beginning of four figures.

They are known as the unfinished slaves. Sculptures by Michelangelo caught midway in the act of their creation[.] They invite us to stand in a masterful moment. The makin[g] of something new.

The past is gone and yet not gone. The future is her[e] and yet not here. We are invited to trust the hands of th[e] master. To live in hope of what these will be.

You don't need to stand in a museum to have this experience. Just open the pages of Scripture.

Jesus comes across men in the most unlikely of places and calls them to follow him. Brothers, mending their fishing nets on the shore. A tax gatherer, sitting behind his booth. In the hands of Jesus, these men would become apostles, witnesses of salvation, and workers in the kingdom of God.

Close the Scriptures, and you can still see God at work today.

In Christ, we have been made God's people. Disciples in his kingdom. This is sure. Certain. His death destroys the power of sin. His resurrection brings life and salvation to you. Yet, we are only beginning to see what we will ultimately be.

We are men of God, under construction.

Look in the mirror and you will catch God midcreation. This is the one he has called. You. Your life is a work of God. He is forming you into the disciple he has called you to be.

Entrust your discipleship into the hands of God. The one who set the stars in the sky knows all that you will be.

O God, my Maker and Redeemer, renew me by your Spirit and equip me for your work. Amen.

FAITH WORKS

When the apostle Paul was in prison, his letters were filled with prayer.

Paul spoke neither in anger at his imprisonment nor in accusation of others. Instead, Paul thanked God for his work in his life and offered petitions for others, even his enemies.

In every circumstance, Paul's life in Christ poured forth in prayer.

Take time this day to pray.

Read a passage of Scripture and identify a teaching from that passage. Let that teaching lead you into prayer.

First, in light of the teaching, confess any failings that come to mind. Then, trusting in Christ, let the teaching guide you to give thanks for some work God has done. Finally, close by letting the teaching lead you to ask something of God, for you, for your loved ones, for the world.

With such prayer, the Word of God will dwell in you richly.

A NOTE FROM THE
AUTHOR

Love the Lord your God with all your heart and with all your soul and with all your mind and with all your strength.
Mark 12:30

When asked which was the greatest commandment, Jesus answered with these words from God, spoken to Israel in the desert (Deuteronomy 6:5).

At the Exodus, God delivered his people from slavery in Egypt. He then sustained them for forty years in the wilderness. As they prepared to enter the Promised Land, God gave them this commandment. Live in love.

God desired his people to enjoy life in a land flowing with milk and honey. The heart of that enjoyment, however, was not the material possessions of the land. It was the spiritual resources of their Lord.

To experience God's love is to experience renewal. To be strengthened in heart, mind, and spirit for service in God's kingdom. You love because you have been loved.

My prayer for you is that these devotions will bring you closer to the heart of God, help you experience his unending love in Christ, and renew you for life.

David R. Schmitt

If this book has made a difference in your life or if you have simply enjoyed it, we would like to hear from you. Your words will encourage us! If you have suggestions for us to consider as we create books like this in the future, please send those, too.

Send e-mail to editor@CTAinc.com and include the subject line: MOG7SC

Write to Editorial Manager, Dept. MOG7SC
CTA, Inc.
PO Box 1205
Fenton, MO 63026-1205

Or leave a product review at www.CTAinc.com (search MOG7SC)